GW00375242

Leo

The Sign of the Lion
July 24–August 23

By Teresa Celsi
and Michael Yawney

Ariel Books

**Andrews McMeel
Publishing**

Kansas City

ISBN: 0-8362-3074-4
Library of Congress Catalog Card Number:
93-73368

Contents

Astrology

An Introduction

E arly in our history, as humankind changed from hunter-gatherers to farmers, they left the forests and moved to the plains, where they could raise plants and livestock. While they guarded their animals at night, the herders gazed up at the sky. They watched the stars circle Earth, counted the days between moons, and perceived an order in the universe.

Astrology was born as a way of finding a meaningful relationship between the movements of the heavens and the events on Earth. Astrologers believe that the celestial dance of planets affects our personalities and destinies. In order to better understand these forces, an astrologer creates a chart, which is like a snapshot of the heavens at the time of your birth. Each planet—Mercury, Venus, Mars, Jupiter, Saturn, Uranus, Neptune, and Pluto—has influence on you. So does the place of your birth.

The most important element in a chart is your sun sign, commonly known as your astrological sign. There are twelve signs of the zodiac, a belt of sky encircling Earth that is divided into twelve zones. Whichever zone the sun was in at your time of birth determines your sun sign. Your sun sign influences conscious behavior. Your moon sign influences unconscious behavior. (This book deals only with sun signs. To find your moon sign, you must look in a reference book or consult an astrologer.)

Each sign is categorized under one of the four elements: *fire, earth, air,* or *water.* Fire signs (Aries, Leo, and Sagittarius) are creative and somewhat self-centered. Earth signs (Taurus, Virgo, and Capricorn) are steady and desire material things. Air signs (Gemini, Libra, and Aquarius) are clever and intellectual.

Water signs (Cancer, Scorpio, and Pisces) are emotional and empathetic.

Each sign has one of three qualities—*cardinal, fixed,* or *mutable*—which shows how it operates. Cardinal signs (Aries, Cancer, Libra, and Capricorn) use their energy to lead in a direct, forceful way. Fixed signs (Taurus, Leo, Scorpio, and Aquarius) harness energy and use it to organize and consolidate. Mutable signs (Gemini, Virgo, Sagittarius, and Pisces) use energy to transform and change.

Every sign has a different combination of an element and a quality. When the positions of all the twelve planets are added to a chart, you can begin to appreciate the complexity of each individual. Astrology does not simplify people by shoving them into twelve personality boxes; rather, the details of your chart will be amazingly complex, inspiring the same awe those early herders must have felt while gazing up into the mystery of the heavens.

The Sign of the Lion

L eo, whose symbol is the Lion, is the embodiment of dignity, pride, and strength. Those born under this sign are dynamic and charismatic, with a natural talent for leadership.

In Greek mythology, Leo is the fierce Nemean lion. Slaying the Nemean lion was the first of the twelve tasks of Hercules. After he had killed the lion, Hercules wore its skin as a trophy and a symbol of his power.

In ancient Egypt, each year when the Sun was in Leo, the Nile rose, fertilizing and enriching the entire flood plain. Leo is ruled by the Sun, the center of our solar system and the giver of life. The Lion is also a sign of nobility and was often used as an emblem by royalty to symbolize its power and position.

Like the Sun, Leo sheds its light and warmth generously on those around it. In return, the Lion asks only one thing: that it be the center of its universe—the brightest star around which everything rotates.

13

Character and Personality

Leo is the monarch of the zodiac. Even if its kingdom is limited to a circle of friends, the Lion commands this circle with love and an authority born of its strong sense of self. This sun sign is aware of its talents and possesses a desire and a need to demonstrate them. It can frequently overwhelm others with its directness, warmth, and generosity.

Leo thrives on the admiration of others—in fact, demands it. The Lion gives a lot and expects a lot in return. Criticism will not be taken lightly by the Lion. After all, the Lion is doing everything to make others happy; how could anyone suggest that things should be done another way?

Leo loves to be at the center of any activity. Whatever this sign does, it does it in the limelight and with flair. You are apt to find the Lion in the trendiest spots in town, surrounded by admirers. Though Leo may naturally stand out in a crowd, it still wants to look better than anyone else. A great deal of time spent in front of the mirror, primping and posing, is common for this sign.

The Lion has a highly developed sense of responsibility and a strong urge to help others; this urge is usually carried out with a Leo-knows-best attitude—the negative side of the Lion's good intentions. Most important, though, the Lion strives to be a shining example of perfection.

Beneath Leo's confident exterior, however, may lurk self-doubts or fears of rejection, which may cause the Lion to indulge its taste for melodrama. The Lion doesn't make gestures, it makes grand gestures. Leo doesn't have troubles, it suffers tragedies. For Leo, expressing its emotions, positive or negative, is essential to its way of life.

Leo is a fixed fire sign. The element of fire denotes creativity; the fixed quality gives the Lion great strength of purpose enabling it to work toward its goals with confidence and determination. This ambition, however, is accompanied by an unyielding will, which Leo must work to control or risk becoming arrogant and bullying. But that's the Lion at its worst; at its best, Leo is like the Sun—warm, giving, and reliable.

Signs and Symbols

E ach sign in the zodiac is ruled by a different planet. Leo is ruled by the Sun, which is the center of our solar system and represents our outward behavior. The Lion, Leo's symbol, figures in many cultures as a symbol of nobility, courage, and power. Tigers as well as lions are associated with this sign.

The fifth sign of the zodiac, Leo combines the element of fire (creativity) with the fixed quality of harnessed energy. Those born under this sign are good-natured, creative, and generous. They are also resolute. When a Lion says "I will," it means it. Loving, courageous, loyal, conceited, bossy—these are all leonine traits.

Leo is linked with Sunday and rules the heart, spine, and back. Its lucky number is nineteen. Red, orange, gold, and yellow are Leo's colors; amber, ruby, and chrysolite are its gemstones; and gold is its metal. Plants and flowers linked with Leo are the yellow lily, poppy, sunflower, and marigold. Its foods are honey, rice, and meat.

Health and Fitness

Most Leos enjoy excellent health, and lead active lives. The Lion positively radiates energy, and since physical appearance is so important to the vain Lion, it works hard to keep fit.

Horseback riding and horsemanship are particularly appealing to this sign. So are team sports like competitive skiing or swimming, where the Lion will be admired for its strength and agility. Look for the social Lion at the gym, too.

Since Leo rules the heart, those born under this sign are most vulnerable when in the throes of a heartache. At these times, the Lion needs attention and sympathy more than medication. Whatever the ailment, they usually bounce back quickly.

Leo loves its pleasures—food being one of them. The Lion must take care not to overindulge its fondness for extravagant meals—one of its ways of showing others it values the luxuries of life. A vibrant sign, Leo needs protein and plenty of fruits and vegetables to replenish its energy.

Home and Family

The Leo home will be palatial—reflecting the Lion's need to impress others with its high standard of living. Furniture and decorations will be on a grand scale, with warm colors and luxurious fabrics. Housework and cooking are usually not part of Leo's repertoire. The monarch prefers to leave these tasks to others—servants, if possible.

Leo loves to entertain. An outgoing and accommodating host, the Lion strives to make each guest feel welcome and comfortable. Even if a Leo party is catered, it will bear the Lion's personal touch with an elaborate array of food and drink to please every taste.

Family is very important to Leo. In particular, those born under this sign adore children and spoil them— treating their children like young royalty. Leo's children are likely to dress in the most fashionable clothes and to play with the most expensive toys.

Careers and Goals

T his fixed fire sign possesses great passion, and tends to express it in public careers, often as an actor or entertainer. Leo is a natural performer, dynamic and charismatic, and basks in the attention of an audience.

Since Leo also wants to be in a position of authority, this sign makes an excellent administrator. Its dramatic flair may even lead it to the pulpit, where it can guide its congregation toward meaningful lives and right action.

Because Leo directs its energy outward, it is intensely interested in other people. When the Lion listens to someone, it gives its undivided attention. This, combined with a drive to help others solve their problems, enables those Leos who choose the psychological professions to work effectively.

Leos also excel in public office. They have the ambition, enthusiasm, and courage to carry out their ideas and principles, as well as a talent for organization and leadership.

Pastimes and Play

Most of the Lion's activities are social rather than solitary. Because it needs the stimulation and admiration of others to feel happy, Leo would rather go to a party than curl up with a good book. For this sign, what it's doing matters more than where it's doing it. If the Lion spends an afternoon at the pool, it's to chat and mingle with the other sunbathers, not to swim.

Leo loves warmth and light, and when the sun goes down, the Lion seeks satisfaction in the glow of neon or candle-light. Whether it's a luxurious dinner at an elegant, new restaurant or partying all night at a trendy club, Leo likes to be out and about—and surrounded by doting friends.

Leos are often artistic, and one of their favorite hobbies is photography. Their flair for the dramatic and their natural talent for putting people at their ease, makes them wonderful portrait photographers—capable of producing exciting and provocative pictures.

Love Among the Signs

W hat is attraction? What is love? Throughout the centuries, science has tried and failed to come up with a satisfying explanation for the mysterious connection between two people.

For the astrologer, the answer is clear. The position of the planets at the time of your birth creates a pattern that influences you throughout your lifetime.

When your pattern meets another person's, the two of you might clash or harmonize.

Why this mysterious connection occurs can be explored only by completing charts for both individuals. But even if the chemistry is there, will it be a happy relationship? Will it last? No one can tell for certain.

Every relationship requires give-and-take, and an awareness of the sun sign relationships can help with this process. The sun sign influences conscious behavior. Does your lover catalog the items in the medicine cabinet? Chances are you have a Virgo on your hands. Do you like to spend your weekends running while your lover wants to play Scrabble? This could be an Aries–Gemini combination.

To discover more about your relationship, find out your lover's sun sign and look under the appropriate combination. You may learn things you had never even suspected.

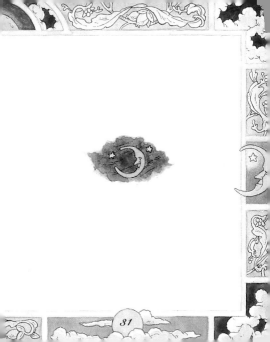

Leo with Aries

(March 21–April 20)

O ther sun signs may tire of the famous Leo need for constant praise and attention. Aries, however, takes it all in stride. The Ram has a large ego itself, and it understands the Lion's needs. Aries admires Leo's creativity and self-possession, and at the same time understands Leo's secret fears. Constant, sincere flattery can help the Lion through those dreaded moments of self-doubt and the Ram will be willing and able to provide it.

Of course, these two will hit some rough spots. The rambunctious Ram doesn't take orders any better than the royal Lion. Nor will the Ram appreciate the free advice Leo so frequently and generously offers. The loving Leo may accuse Aries of being too casual about their relationship and the Ram may respond in a way that offends the Lion's pride. However, flare-ups between these two will be brief since Leo and Aries enjoy each other too much to spend a lot of time arguing.

Leo is likely to want a commitment sooner than Aries. Once in love, the

Lion wants to settle down and make a home. But the Ram is a rover, always looking to see what's coming over the horizon. Should Aries decide to commit, however, the Ram will proceed with its customary enthusiasm. Like the Lion, Aires genuinely loves children and can play happily with them for hours. Discipline will be difficult for these two. Leo may lecture a bit and provide some guidelines but neither sign will be too stern as a parent.

As business partners, Leo and Aries are well suited. They respect and admire each other and they attract talented, loyal employees; together they can generate the kinds of ideas that can take a business into the Fortune 500. However, neither is at all practical with money: They like to spend, not save. If they can break this habit, their partnership could prosper.

Both these amorous fire signs want and appreciate a touch of tenderness in a partner. Leo, however, needs much more than mere affection. The Lion wants to be adored—in bed and out. Aries will provide the adoration if Leo will curb its tendency to dominate.

Both signs are givers, and with each contributing its best to the other, the Lion and the Ram can look forward to a strong, fulfilling relationship.

Leo with Taurus
(April 21–May 21)

aurus, the Bull, is an earth sign whose practicality and tenacity might seem to make it an unlikely partner for the flamboyant, enthusiastic Leo. In fact, the emotional needs of these two signs are remarkably similar. Like Leo, Taurus craves love and the appreciation of others, although the Bull may not admit it as readily as the Lion.

Leo, like all fire signs, is ready, willing, and able to give Taurus all the love it needs. Taurus will return the love in equal amounts, but not in the openly affectionate manner that the Lion prefers. Unfortunately for Leo, earth signs dislike drawing attention to themselves.

The Bull's shyness can be a boon to the Lion, however. Any recognition or awards for the work done by this team will go to the Lion. Leo can make all the public appearances; Taurus will watch from the sidelines, satisfied to have contributed to a job well done.

Every relationship has its ups and downs. With Taurus and Leo, they stem from the Bull's possessiveness and the Lion's impatience. The shy Bull genuinely admires Leo's charisma, yet in social situations the Bull can become extremely jealous of the attention the Lion receives—especially when the openly flirtatious Lion is always the center of attention.

To reassure Taurus, Leo must give the Bull plenty of physical proof of its affection. Both signs are capable of initiating lovemaking, but it is more likely to be Taurus, since the proud Leo prefers to be courted. Direct, passionate advances from Leo would give Taurus the security it needs and help keep its jealousy at bay—something the willful Lion should consider.

That still leaves Leo's impatience as

an obstacle to harmony between these two. The Lion's ambitious nature compels it to try to conquer the world in an instant. Leo is a risk taker, willing to stake everything on the big payoff. Taurus is a plodder, preferring to work slowly and steadily toward its goals. This style, so alien to the Lion's, will test Leo's patience. However, if the Lion can accept the Bull's systematic approach, it will discover that, no matter what the pace, going places with the Bull is bound to be a pleasure.

Leo with Gemini
(May 22–June 21)

These two signs can enjoy each other's company for hours. Gemini, the sign of the Twins, is one of the most inventive, quick-witted, and expressive signs of the zodiac, able to change its personality in a flash. Leo loves a crowd, and Gemini seems to be a crowd all in one person.

Leo will soon learn, however, that beneath this mercurial façade, Gemini has a deep need for stability and a calm, quiet place where it can replenish itself. Leo, although it loves the social whirl, is at its best when dealing with people on a one-to-one basis. The Lion instinctively knows the needs of others and can create the stable environment Gemini is seeking.

The Twins need mental stimulation from a variety of people. Gemini is a sign of communication and creative expression. It will want to spend time away from Leo, interacting with others and exchanging ideas. Leo is apt to take this behavior as a personal affront. The Lion wants and needs to be at the center of its mate's universe and will have trouble accepting the fact that Gemini can enjoy itself when the Lion is not around.

The physical relationship between Leo and Gemini can be tricky. Leo is a generous and enthusiastic lover; sex is a passionate expression of its love and affection. Gemini, on the other hand, is likely to withdraw if lovemaking gets too serious. Playful and lighthearted lovemaking is what the Twins prefer. What's more, variety is not the Lion's forte, and Gemini can become easily bored by the same old routine, no matter how passionate. In order to keep the Twins interested, Leo will have to be more willing to experiment and let Gemini take the lead in the bedroom.

A successful business partnership between Leo and Gemini is rare. Both lack the drive necessary to start a business or the ambition to make it thrive. They need the stabilizing influence of a third party (preferably an earth sign, such as Taurus) to provide a proper foundation for any business venture.

Nevertheless, in friendship or marriage, Leo's warmth and strength can provide the stability the Twins need, and Gemini's imagination and playfulness can prevent the Lion from becoming stodgy and set in its ways.

Leo with Cancer

(June 22–July 23)

The typical Cancer, whose symbol is the Crab, wants to nurture and care for others, a trait that should fit well with Leo. Cancer lives to love; Leo lives to be loved.

There are problems, however. Although Cancer admires Leo's energy and resolution, the Crab is not given to idle praise and flattery. Instead, it demonstrates its love with sympathy and protectiveness. Leo, however, doesn't need protection; it needs adoration.

Tensions might arise when Leo tries to deal with Cancer's emotional ups and downs. A water sign ruled by the Moon, Cancer is highly sensitive to its emotional environment and can change moods very quickly and often retreats into its shell when confronted with problems. Leo's first instinct would be to try to solve Cancer's problems. However, what Cancer really needs is a sympathetic hug and a steady partner who isn't put off by its uncontrollable moodiness.

As lovers, both signs are passionate, but each has a different approach. Leo views lovemaking as an expression of its power and sexuality. Cancer wants emotions and sentiment—the courtly trappings of love and all the tokens of affection. Unless the Lion and the Crab make allowances for these differences, a deeply satisfying romantic relationship will be difficult to sustain.

The Lion and the Crab are the parents of the zodiac—and they excel in these roles. Even when it has a demanding career, Cancer will be deeply involved with home and family. The Crab is at its best when tending to family members and maintaining harmony in the home. Leo is at its best when offering advice or setting an example.

In business, these two signs can build an empire if each contributes according to its strengths. Leo will bring the energy, the ambition, and the creative ideas; Cancer will provide the financial savvy and interpersonal skills.

It won't be difficult for this partnership to succeed; their differences are not crucial and can be easily compensated for. The Lion can learn a strange and wonderful truth from the Crab: True love and admiration from one person can be as good as or better than the adoration of millions.

Leo with Leo

(July 24–August 23)

I t has been said that marriage is like a garden: one partner is the gardener, the other is the flowers. One nurtures while the other blooms. The problem when two Leos come together is that neither wants to be the gardener—only the flowers.

Nevertheless, two Leos can share an exciting and fun-filled friendship. Both like to socialize and appreciate a dynamic partner who exudes energy and warmth. One Leo will also understand the other's need for constant applause. Confidence and trust are the hallmarks of a Leo–Leo friendship. These two will take comfort in each other's approval, as well.

Control is the big stumbling block with these two. In a marriage or as lovers, friction is inevitable if neither will submit. No Lion, however, will be happy in the shadow of another, so submission will only lead to more frustration and conflict. And once in power, no self-respecting Leo would willingly hand over the crown.

In business, too, it is not a good idea for two Leos to form a partnership. Both are creative entrepreneurs with wonderful luck and brilliant prospects. Typically, however, both want to be in charge. Unless they can divide their responsibilities so that each is in control of a separate area, any business venture is bound to flounder.

The solution lies in separate kingdoms. For instance, if these two have different occupations, they will be much more compatible when it comes to other aspects of their relationship. They can even help each other with advice and support, provided these are given without criticism.

In spite of the obstacles, love can conquer all in this relationship. Leos live for love and admiration and are capable of giving them as well. Their physical relationship will be an ardent mix of passion and tenderness. Lovemaking may get off to a slow start, since pride may demand that the other make the first move. Once past this obstacle, however, life in the bedroom will be exciting and fulfilling since both signs enjoy the same style and have the same expectations.

The key to this relationship is for each partner to sacrifice some pride. That accomplished, there will be peace in the kingdom.

Leo with Virgo

(August 24–September 23)

With Leo and Virgo it's seldom love at first sight. In fact, love may never enter the picture. But if it does, it will be a hard-won victory.

Virgo sees the world from an analytical point of view. The Virgin is only comfortable with an idea or a situation once it has taken it apart, viewed it from all angles, then put it back together again. It scrutinizes people in the same way—analyzing their virtues and faults—and then openly expressing the results of its study. This approach can be poison to the self-centered and proud Lion. Any suggestion of imperfection will damage the Lion's self-esteem. And the Lion is not particularly responsive to the analytical approach; it relies on creativity rather than logic to see it through.

When these two come into conflict, each sign has its own line of defense. For the Virgin, it's disapproval—something the Lion can't abide. For Leo, it's the sheer force of its personality. When the Lion feels thwarted or insecure, it simply emits an intimidating roar and demands to have its own way.

However, the Virgin is not easily intimidated—nor is it swept off its feet by the Lion's charisma. What will impress this sign is the Lion's strength, loyalty, and generosity.

As business partners, these two signs complement each other. Virgo is practical, efficient, and economical, and possesses the concentration and capacity for hard work necessary to implement Leo's creative schemes.

In lovemaking, Leo may feel that Virgo is too tentative—but the Lion should refrain from demanding too much too soon. Leo's optimistic nature and warm personality could light the cool Virgo's hidden fires—provided the Lion is patient and gentle. If not, the Virgin's critical nature could surface and quickly destroy the mood.

Whether or not these two can work things out will depend upon the Lion's adaptability and the Virgin's restraint. Though the Virgin won't indulge the Lion with idle praise, it could learn to be less critical and more tactful. And, hard as it might be, the vain Lion could learn to live without constant flattery. What the Virgin has to offer is love and loyalty. The Lion must decide if those will suffice.

Leo with Libra

(September 24–October 23)

W hen Leo issues a royal command, the Lion expects to be obeyed at once. However, if the command is given to the Scales, Leo had better lower its expectations. To Libra, a decree is not something to be acted on; it is a proposition offered for debate.

Libra is a cardinal air sign whose symbol is the Scales. As one might expect, the sign of the Scales is especially concerned with relationship, harmony, and balance. When all sides of an issue are considered and weighed, and the proper equilibrium is attained, this sign is content. Unfortunately, these same concerns often make Libra appear vacillating and somewhat superficial.

For a forthright, decisive Leo, this systematic approach to problem solving can be annoying. But Libra has the capacity to dispel discord and disagreement. An accomplished diplomat, the sign of the Scales presents its ideas so smoothly that it is difficult to take offense. Libra avoids discord with the Lion by gently reminding Leo that there is more than one side to an argument. Leo is not likely to mind this, as long as any ultimate decisions are left to the Lion.

Libra, like Leo, is a social sign. The sign of the Scales is friendly with everyone and always tries to find something good in the people it meets. Leo may wish Libra weren't quite so popular. The Lion's jealous streak can flair up when it sees Libra surrounded by a circle of admiring fans. Libra seldom succumbs to jealousy, an emotion it finds disagreeable, and will not mind it when the Lion is the center of attention.

As lovers or spouses, Libra and Leo both enjoy extravagant gestures and look for impressive ways to say "I love you." Libra has excellent taste and will make their home a showplace worthy of the Lion's pride and vanity. Leo will have to be patient, however, because Libra will not be satisfied until the perfect spot is found for every object and the entire house reflects a harmonious balance.

Libra is a romantic, but not an overtly passionate one. Leo will have to go slowly and patiently to draw out the Scales. In turn, Libra will give Leo the harmony, balance, and beauty its kingdom needs.

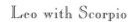

Leo with Scorpio

(October 24–November 22)

L eo is likely to be drawn to the mysterious and seductive Scorpio at first sight. Scorpio, whose symbol is the Scorpion, is probably the most sexually magnetic sign of the zodiac. A romance between these two will be on the scale of a grand passion.

Each will insist on total devotion from the other. The monarch Leo abhors disloyalty, and Scorpio wants to completely possess those it desires. Fortunately, each sign is capable of fulfilling the other's needs. Leo's passion and intensity are well suited to Scorpio's engrossing and seemingly bottomless love. Sexually, both bring a dynamic energy and passion to lovemaking. Scorpio, who often exerts superhuman control over its feelings, will find emotional liberation possible with the warm and loving Lion.

With common goals, their love could last a lifetime. Without them, their relationship could turn hostile. The problem is a lack of flexibility—both are fixed signs who will neither relent nor reform. In any relationship, monarch Leo must be the dominant partner, while Scorpio cannot relinquish control of any aspect of its life. This comes from the Scorpion's deep-seated need to protect itself. If opposed or hurt, the Scorpion will mete out revenge, even if the offending deed is long past and forgotten by the perpetrator. This behavior bewilders the Lion and, puzzled and hurt, it will lash out. Having a shared goal will give them an opportunity to air grievances and to work together at problem solving.

Leo and Scorpio can be business partners, but it will take some effort. Scorpio will allow Leo to do the front work, but the Scorpion will insist on making the decisions. With Leo providing the star quality and Scorpio the strategy, this could be a winning combination. Unfortunately, the partnership is more than likely to become a power struggle, with neither giving in to the other's will to dominate.

Despite some seemingly impossible obstacles, Leo and Scorpio are irresistibly attracted to each other. Either the attraction will grow into fierce dislike, or it will lead to a deeply rewarding relationship. If Leo can adjust to a mate who refuses to stroke its inflated ego, it might find instead a mate whose devotion knows no limits.

Leo with Sagittarius
(November 23–December 21)

B oth fire signs, Leo and Sagittarius share a common outlook on life. Sagittarius, whose sign is the Archer, is ruled by Jupiter, symbol of optimism and enthusiasm. Like Leo, the Archer is a social creature who thrives on activity and the attention of others. Leo's energy is a little less frenetic, however. While the Lion is often content to just bask in the sun, Sagittarius is restless, both physically and mentally, sometimes to the point of recklessness. Together, however, these two signs can be wonderful friends and partners.

In business, the dreamy Archer is capable of brilliant, if sometimes wild, schemes though it often lacks the ability to see its ideas through. The Lion, on the other hand, is a terrific organizer and formidable administrator who can help the Archer carry projects through to completion. One caution, however: Neither sign is too practical in money matters so their partnership needs someone else to guide and manage their financial affairs.

Some of Sagittarius's traits can drive

Leo up the wall. For one thing, Sagittarius rarely does what it is told. Ask the Archer to buy a dozen eggs at the store, and it might bring home two pounds of tofu instead. Ask why, and the answer may be painfully frank. The Archer might tell Leo its cholesterol count is high enough, and besides, the Lion could stand to lose a few pounds.

This frankness won't be appreciated by Leo, especially when the implication is that the Lion is somehow less than perfect. But Sagittarius, unlike other signs, can get away with an occasional criticism of the Lion. Its disposition is so sunny and so witty that it's easy for Leo to overlook small indiscretions.

However, Leo won't be as willing to overlook the Archer's flirtations. To Sagittarius, flirting is acceptable social behavior and the implications of its actions are no cause for concern. However, what the Archer views as friendly fun, Leo sees as an open invitation.

Still, these obstacles pale when compared to the many things these fire signs share. If Leo will give Sagittarius the measure of freedom this dreamer needs, and Sagittarius will be content to let Leo rule the kingdom, all will be well.

Leo with Capricorn
(December 22–January 20)

The Lion works hard and is successful in most endeavors. It plays hard, too, and is just as successful in attracting new friends as it is in attracting business associates. Capricorn, on the other hand, doesn't always know when to relax. This earth sign, symbolized by the Goat, is the embodiment of order, structure, and sobriety. For the Goat, there is always some work to be done, some goal to be achieved.

The Goat envies the Lion's ability to attract others, seemingly with little effort. Capricorn's problem is that it tends to project an air of critical superiority— not a trait likely to draw people in its direction. However, the Goat is not being critical of others; it is merely appraising them in order to discover their most useful attributes. Leo, on the other hand, envies Capricorn's discipline, even if it doesn't quite believe that the Goat would rather work than play.

Each of these signs has the ability to uncover and utilize people's hidden talents. Can they do the same for each other? Down-to-earth Capricorn can help Leo focus its energy and creativity into practical and useful channels. And the charismatic Lion can introduce the Goat to people who wouldn't previously have found their way past its stand-offishness.

Marriage and a stable home life is as important to Capricorn as it is to Leo. As parents, they are steady, if stern. The Lion, who likes to lead by example, will be more indulgent, often relaxing the rules Capricorn finds so hard to bend. Both parents, however, will expect their children to work hard, maintain high grades and excel in extracurricular activities.

Capricorn is not a sign of raging passion. Should Leo expect great enthusiasm, it is likely to be disappointed. Nevertheless, the Goat possesses a powerful but latent sensuality, and if the Lion is not overwhelming, these feelings will surface—to the delight of both partners. But if Capricorn is intimidated, it may become judgmental—a sure way to send the Lion packing.

If Leo can pierce Capricorn's reserve and aloof exterior, the Lion will discover the Goat's good humor, affection, and loyalty—all traits the Lion shares. This could be a match made in heaven.

Leo with Aquarius

(January 21–February 19)

In the circle of the zodiac, Leo and Aquarius are opposite each other. Each opposing sign usually possesses qualities the other lacks. Leo and Aquarius are both outgoing and share the need for lots of company—but here their similarities end.

Like Leo, Aquarius is a fixed sign. But its element is air, and it is ruled by Uranus, the planet of the unexpected. Spontaneous, curious, idealistic, and revolutionary, the Water Bearer's destiny is to shake up the world.

Aquarius loves stimulating ideas and free-flowing conversations, and it tends to have friends from all walks of life. Open and spontaneous, the Water Bearer needs to be free from restrictions. These traits often lead this sign to break traditional rules of conduct while pursuing its idealistic goals. Aquarius can be disruptive and unpredictable and, in some cases, downright eccentric.

Leo is an aristocrat with a strong allegiance to the status quo. The Lion surrounds itself with admiring friends from whom it demands and receives adulation. For Leo, individual needs transcend

73

any grand utopian schemes for improving the lot of the masses.

Putting aside their differences will be difficult for these two signs. The Water Bearer is simply not going to waste its time boosting the Lion's ego. Aquarius is driven to improve the world and it generally looks more for what is wrong than for what is right—not a quality Leo wants in a mate.

Marriage is likely to be fraught with tension and conflict. Aquarius will be indifferent to Leo's need to be pampered and adored. And Leo will interpret the Water Bearer's inattention in a negative way— as an uncaring spouse who is more interested in others than in the Lion.

As lovers, Aquarius might be too experimental for Leo. The Lion prefers power to diversity. Aquarius will not be dominated by any individual and is likely to become cool and distant when Leo tries. Eventually Aquarius will tire of Leo's domineering behavior, and Leo will look elsewhere for adoration.

Like most opposites, these two could learn from each other if they wanted to. From Leo, the Water Bearer could discover the pleasure to be derived from a committed relationship; and from Aquarius, the Lion could discover what it means to commit to a cause larger than itself.

Leo with Pisces

(February 20–March 20)

Being with a Pisces is a rather odd relationship for Leo. The Lion usually expects the service of others and accepts that as its due. With Pisces, however, Leo is the one who serves, providing protection and security. This pairing is rather like the relationship of the patron to the artist.

A mutable water sign, symbolized by the Fish, Pisces relates more to the world of dreams and emotions than to the world of practical matters. Although Leo cannot completely enter this mystical world, the Lion recognizes the importance of this realm and will help provide what is necessary for the Fish to explore it. This often entails doing things for the Fish it would never consider doing for other signs of the zodiac.

Spirituality and mysticism come naturally to Pisces, who is quite at home with dreams and shadows, half-glimpsed truths and illusions. Pisces may be so busy dreaming that life's mundane activities, like paying the light bill or shopping for groceries, are completely overlooked. In fact, the Fish sometimes has difficulty focusing on the here and now and may tend toward escapism.

In this relationship, Leo, although extravagant and reluctant to take on everyday chores, will be the one to keep track of practical matters. The Lion, however, would be wise to consult the Fish on major financial matters. Pisces is creative with money and may come up with an idea that Leo would never think of.

Leo will lure the Fish with its warmth, charm, and creative power. And once reeled in, Pisces will admire Leo's strength and boldness. To vulnerable and sensitive Pisces, Leo offers a reliable and unshakable foundation.

However, Leo's intense personality

can be overwhelming to Pisces. The Lion can dominate to the point of bullying, and often relies on its partner to let it know when it has gone too far. But Pisces hates confrontation and usually will swim away to avoid a fight. Leo may not realize how much damage has been done until it is too late.

Leo could not find a more sensitive, appreciative audience than the empathetic Pisces. If Leo will only tone down its domineering behavior, the Fish will readily swim into its warm waters—and stay there happy and secure.

The text of this book was set in Bembo
and the display in Caslon Open Face
by Crane Typesetting Service, Inc.,
West Barnstable, Massachusetts.

Book design and illustrations by
JUDITH A. STAGNITTO